After-School
FUN

Swimming

by JoAnn Early Macken

Reading consultant: Susan Nations, M.Ed., author/literacy coach/consultant

WR WEEKLY READER
EARLY LEARNING LIBRARY

Please visit our web site at: www.earlyliteracy.cc
For a free color catalog describing Weekly Reader® Early Learning Library's list
of high-quality books, call 1-877-445-5824 (USA) or 1-800-387-3178 (Canada).
Weekly Reader® Early Learning Library's fax: (414) 336-0164.

Library of Congress Cataloging-in-Publication Data

Macken, JoAnn Early, 1953-
    Swimming / by JoAnn Early Macken.
        p. cm. — (After-school fun)
    Includes bibliographical references and index.
    ISBN 0-8368-4516-1 (lib. bdg.)
    ISBN 0-8368-4523-4 (softcover)
    1. Swimming—Juvenile literature. I. Title.
GV837.6.M33   2005
797.2'1—dc22   2004061172

This edition first published in 2005 by
Weekly Reader® Early Learning Library
330 West Olive Street, Suite 100
Milwaukee, WI 53212 USA

Photographer: Gregg Andersen
Picture research: Diane Laska-Swanke
Art direction and page layout: Tammy West

Printed in the United States of America

1 2 3 4 5 6 7 8 9 09 08 07 06 05

Note to Educators and Parents

Reading is such an exciting adventure for young children! They are beginning to integrate their oral language skills with written language. To encourage children along the path to early literacy, books must be colorful, engaging, and interesting; they should invite the young reader to explore both the print and the pictures.

After-School Fun is a new series designed to help children read about the kinds of activities they enjoy in their free time. In each book, young readers learn about a different artistic endeavor, physical activity, or learning experience.

Each book is specially designed to support the young reader in the reading process. The familiar topics are appealing to young children and invite them to read — and reread — again and again. The full-color photographs and enhanced text further support the student during the reading process.

In addition to serving as wonderful picture books in schools, libraries, homes, and other places where children learn to love reading, these books are specifically intended to be read within an instructional guided reading group. This small group setting allows beginning readers to work with a fluent adult model as they make meaning from the text. After children develop fluency with the text and content, the book can be read independently. Children and adults alike will find these books supportive, engaging, and fun!

— Susan Nations, M.Ed., author, literacy coach, and consultant in literacy development

After school, I go to swim club. I meet my friends at the pool. I wear my swimsuit.

Goggles help me see in the water. They help protect my eyes, too. A cap keeps my hair out of my eyes.

Our coach tells us the safety rules. We stretch our arms and legs on the deck. We stretch to warm up for swimming.

We learn the freestyle stroke, or front crawl. We practice kicking with kickboards. We learn the flutter kick.

We learn how to pull with our arms. My hands reach into the water and push it back behind me.

We learn how to breathe while we swim. I turn my head to one side and take a breath. I breathe out in the water. I am swimming!

We play a game in the pool. Our coach throws a ring into the water. We dive to the bottom and bring it back.

Our club goes to a swim meet. The swimmers dive into the water. They race across the pool. Each swimmer swims in a lane.

The swimmers turn at the end of the pool. The first one back wins the race. We cheer for our team. Hooray!

3 FT 6 IN

Glossary

goggles — glasses that fit close to the face

kickboards — boards that swimmers hold while they practice kicks. A kickboard helps a swimmer float.

meet — a sports event with many races or contests

stroke — arm and leg movements

For More Information

Books

Elephants Swim. Linda Capus Riley (Houghton Mifflin)

Get Set! Swim! Jeannine Atkins (Lee & Low)

Swim! Eve Rice (Greenwillow)

Swimming. Cynthia Klingel and Robert B. Noyed (Child's World)

Web Sites

Pool Kids USA
www.poolkidsusa.com/
Swimming safety tips, pool games, puzzles

Index

About the Author

JoAnn Early Macken is the author of two rhyming picture books, *Sing-Along Song* and *Cats on Judy*, and six other series of nonfiction books for beginning readers. Her poems have appeared in several children's magazines. A graduate of the M.F.A. in Writing for Children and Young Adults program at Vermont College, she lives in Wisconsin with her husband and their two sons. Visit her Web site at www.joannmacken.com.